No name

Just Angels!

Copyright © 2023 by Claudia Boymouchakian

All rights reserved. No part of this book may be reproduced by any mechanical, photographic, or electronic process, or in the form of a phonographic recording, nor may it be stored in a retrieval system, transmitted, or otherwise be copied for public or private use, or used in any manner without written permission of the copyright owner except for the use of quotations in a book review.

The author of this book does not offer medical advice or prescribe the use of any technique as a form of treatment for physical, emotional, mental, or medical problems without the advice of a physician and medical professional, either directly or indirectly. The intent of the author is only to offer information of a general nature to help you in your quest for spiritual wellbeing. In the event you use any of the information in this book for yourself, the author and the publisher assume no responsibility for your actions.

FIRST EDITION, 15th DECEMBER 2023

www.purpleangelhealing.com.au

ISBN: 978-0-6459817-1-1

No name

Just Angels!

Angel words whispered by my Guardian Angels,

Archangels and Higher Beings of Light

From the Celestial Realm…

… to help you heal and enjoy your Life!

CLAUDIA BOYMOUCHAKIAN

Table of Contents

How did I receive these whispers in my ears? 1

Chapter 1: We are Here. You are Here 6

Chapter 2: Smile. Honour your Life 15

Chapter 3: Listen in Silence 21

Chapter 4: Connect – We are One 26

Chapter 5: A message from Blue Angel 31

Chapter 6: Live your Life with Red Passion 40

Chapter 7: Trust and Change 45

Chapter 8: Draw your Dreams 51

Chapter 9: Intuition – Gratitude - Love 56

Chapter 10: Regain your power! Angel wings box 63

Chapter 11: Rainbow Angel wants to join you today 69

Chapter 12: Angel Colours 73

Chapter 13: Green Angel, Healing Angel 80

Chapter 14: You know this one… Purple Angel! 85

Chapter 15: I am here… don't be afraid 89

Chapter 16: An Angel from the Sea 93

Chapter 17: Your essence: Freedom, Joy & Love 97

Chapter 18: Allow the messages in 105

Chapter 19: Expand your heart 109

Chapter 20: Walking with you… always 115

Final words 120

About the author 123

How did I receive these whispers in my ears?

December 2011. The first weekend of this month I joined Doreen Virtue on her Angel Intuitive® course in Coolum (Queensland, Australia). It was an amazing, heart-opening and mind-blowing weekend! I learnt to TRUST! Trust the Angels, trust myself and trust their Guidance and connection!

With the high energies still in my heart, I returned to Sydney incredibly happy, connected and euphoric!

Two days later, I received a call from Argentina informing me that my mother was very sick, and bed bound. I knew she was sick… She had been sick for years and years. Her ESSENCE, though, was stronger than her body for such a long time… But not this time. She was getting ready to go back Home.

Without hesitation, I took the next flight to Argentina. Of course, my mother was waiting for me ☺. My friend Monica told me a few times: "Every time you come back home, your mother revives". That is **LOVE**.

Why am I telling you this? Because my mother, Anahid, was a great supporter of my intuitive work! Because this was an important step in my Life, and it was during this experience that I started really trusting, paying attention and listening to the Angels' whispers that created this book.

During the Angel Intuitive training, one of the participants told me that I was going to "write a book on green paper with a green pen". "Oh, yeah!" I thought. And I added, "Angels, show me how".

I did not quite believe this message. How would you read words written with *green ink* on a *green paper*? ☺

Well, when I arrived at my home-town Mar del Plata (Argentina), on my mother's dining room table there was a block of… A4 green papers that I had bought on one of my trips to Brazil many, many years ago. I had left this block of papers in a drawer when I moved to Australia. My mum told me that she was not going to use those papers and that I could have them back if I wished…

Well… here is my green paper! Happily, I took these green papers to the office-shop and had them cut in halves and bound.

The next day, I showed my mum the 'new notebooks' and she said that she had lots of pens in a pencil box that I could take with me as she wasn't going to use them. In fact, there were not a lot of pens, but… there was one Green Pen! Bingo!

"A green pen and a green notebook". Here we go!

I also had taken with me on that trip, my crystals and my magick blanket gifted to me by my dearest husband (which I carry everywhere I go). That night, I sat on my bed to meditate and… that was when I started 'listening' the Angels' whispers…

They told me to get the pen and the notebook, to TRUST and start writing!

It has been a long time since then... More than ten years.

I painted the angels for this book, and my friend gifted me one of hers... the Golden Angel!

After a long journey... finally, here is the book!

For you to enjoy, to start trusting your Angels, to know and feel that they are always here for you... You only need to ASK for their assistance and they will be there!

At the end of each chapter, there is an invitation to do, write, draw, colour or do something special. This is your time to go within and have fun with the Angels! Trust the process. Do not judge yourself. Enjoy the unfolding!

Sending Love and a thousand Angels to you,

Claudia Boymouchakian

I dedicate this book to my beloved mother, Anahid Abachian de Boymouchakian, who always supported my dreams, who gave me wings to fly and who always loved me, and still loves me, now from the Other Side, where she is probably having great chats and lots of fun with the Angels!

My mum and me, 1967

Chapter 1

We are Here. You are Here

Have you ever listened to that soft whisper in your ear saying "I love you"?

Have you ever dreamed you were flying high, remarkably high, without any fear?

Have you ever felt the warmth of the Sun in your heart?

Have you ever dropped a tear in front of a sunrise, a sunset… or a baby?

Yes, I am sure you did! You probably felt many more moments with your heart and your Soul.

I want to tell you that you are not the only one. You are not alone!

Millions of people are awakening in this moment to a new consciousness, to an open heart. They are realising that We Are One, and only through this connecting feeling we can all achieve Peace on Earth.

When every human being lives in a small (and big at the same time!) place of Peace in their hearts, is when Peace on Earth will manifest, increase and multiply and then Peace will finally surround our beautiful Planet.

Find Peace in every situation in your Life.

Find Peace in each moment you are present.

Find Peace in your heart… in your home…

Find Peace in every interaction with others during your daily activities.

There will be a place of Peace very soon…

Elevate your frequency.

Cultivate Peace.

Love is Peace.

Peace is Love.

Peace is IN your Heart.

Love all forms of Life.

Honour Life in plants, animals, minerals… not only in human beings.

Love your Life for *this* is what you are here for… now.

Learn. Grow. Experience. Live. Love.

Now is the Time.

Time to Live.

Time to Love.

Time of Peace.

The shift occurring in our beloved Planet Earth is allowing you to Live your Life with Love and Peace to its fullest! Take the leap!

Accept what you are going through now, for this is what will make you grow your Spirit and value your human experience in this Life. And learn…

Remember: You are a Sparkle of Divine Light.

You can create the Life you desire.

You are Divine Light.

Shine. Love. Live!

Shine in every situation.

Shine wherever you are.

Shine alone… and surrounded by people.

Just Shine. Love. Live.

Keep in mind you are a Sparkle of Divine Light.

Keep Shining… and you will be living in Peace and teaching others to be in Peace. Sharing the Light. Sharing the Love. Sharing Life.

Be mindful of your words as they create your reality.

Use only positive, uplifting, inspiring, loving words… for you and for others.

Fill your words with Love.

Surround your words with Peace.

Wrap your words with a ribbon of Light and let them elevate to the Universe to create your reality.

Be positive.

Stay calm.

Trust.

There is a group of Higher Beings in the Light that is ready to help you if you ask for help.

Ascended Masters, God/Goddess, Angels and Archangels are ready to answer your prayers. You only need to ASK.

Trust

Love

Live

Ask

Receive!

Connect with Crystals.

Learn their attributes and how they can assist you.

Play with crystals. Embrace their colours. Colour your Life. Trust.

Feel the energies that different crystals emanate. Feel them deeply. Feel the energy in your body, in your heart, in your Soul. They are here to help you heal and help others heal. Connect.

Crystals

Colours

Energies

Healing

Lightworkers are here to support your learning and your growing path.

Ask. Read. Heal. Connect. Trust.

You can develop your healing abilities to their maximum potential.

Trust

Learn

Experience

Smile!

You are a Lightworker!

Connecting with your Angels

In this page, write loving words and then draw a big ribbon with a colour that represents "Light" to you.

Create a 'package' with your words and the ribbon around them. Then ask your angels to send these words, their energy, to the Universe.

Share the Light! Share your Love!

Date:

Chapter 2

Smile. Honour your Life

Smile! Just Smile!

Let your smile be present in your heart, in your life, in your days and nights.

Sometimes you may encounter yourself immersed in situations where it will be difficult to smile. Smile anyway!

If you smile *in* your Heart, nothing can make you sad. Your Inner Smile is your most powerful tool to stay and to be happy, balanced, centered. No one can touch it!

You only have to smile and let God and the Universe do the rest. Oh… and the angels, of course! They know how to help you!

Your smile will balance and brighten not only your Inner World but also your outer world ☺

Smile
Balance
Inner World

Fill your Inner World with caring, loving, calming words.

Your words create your life.

Say loving words to yourself.

If your Inner World is bright, supportive and happy, so will be your Life.

Be yourself. At all times. Open your loving Heart and show your Balance and your Smile to the world!

Stand up
Stay balanced
Open your Heart
Ground yourself

Feel the energy in your hands, in your feet, in your heart.

You ARE ALIVE!

Honour your Life

Honour all Life

Open your Heart and ground yourself. Take a walk in the forest, feel the grass below your feet. Smell the green air into your lungs. Fill your Heart with fresh, green healing energy. Touch the plants…

Or go to the sea! Take your shoes off and play with the waves. Wet your feet, your legs, your hands… or your whole body! Walk in the sea, dance, jump, skip, sing, swim!

Feel the blue water cleansing you.

Feel your Heart and your Soul with clear, strengthening blue water.

… Or just lie on the ground and look at the clouds! Play with them. Guess their shapes and their messages. Play 'Cloud-Watching'! It's fun!

Imagine yourself in the middle of the most beautiful white cloud. Float with it. Touch it. Embrace the White Light. Fill your Heart with White Loving Light. Be the cloud. Let your Soul shake in happiness. Breathe deeply. Close your eyes. Relax. Enjoy.

Enjoy

Enjoy Life

Enjoy the Colours

Colour in your Life with bright, healing colours.

Let the colours guide and surround you.

What's your favourite colour? Why?

Dress in that colour. Wear adornments of that colour. Fill your spaces with your favourite colour.

Find the meaning and energies of your colour and develop a friendship with it. You are part of it.

You are a colour.

A colourful Spark of Divine Light.

Connecting with the angels… I painted this one!

Connecting with your Angels

Today, find a photo of yourself that you like.

Look at yourself in the photo. What stands out? What are the colours of your clothes? Why do you like the photo? How do you *feel* when you look at yourself in this photo?

1. Print the photo.
2. Glue your photo to this page.
3. Today wear clothes of the same colour you are wearing in the photo. If you don't have any, find an accessory (scarf, earrings, bracelets, hairclip, tie, belt) and wear it.
4. Ask your Guardian Angel to walk before you onto this day!

Date:

Chapter 3

Listen in Silence

There is a time when we all feel that something is missing in our Life.

You search everywhere, but you still feel incomplete. And you will feel incomplete until you start searching inside.

Inside yourself
You will find the answers,
The path, the guide,
That you are looking for
Then, you will feel Complete.

Complete in Love
Complete in Harmony
Complete within YOU

Within you resides all the answers you are searching for. Stay in silence. Meditate. Walk in the forest. Look at the plants. Hug a tree. Roll on the grass. Swim in the water. Listen to music. Or just sit and breathe....

In any of these simple moments, in connection with yourself, you are opening the connection with the Celestial Realm, and we can give you the answers.

Breathe the air. Smell the sea breeze. Look at a bird's flight. Relax.

In this silence, you will find the answers.

We -your angels- will answer your questions.

We will guide, protect, encourage and support you.

We love you and we are here to assist you in finding your answers, your Life Purpose, your Joy, your Love.

Listen to the sounds of Nature.

Make the tunes resonate in your Heart.

Vibrate with the notes and the silence.

In that moment you will feel Our Presence in your heart, and we will pour the answers onto you.

Breathe deeply. Smile Trust.

You are not alone. If you seek you will find us – your Angels, the angels! We are not hiding. We are by your side, awaiting your call to help you and guide you.

Listen in Silence.
Silence is Life.
Silence is God.
Silence is YOU.

Enjoy the Silence for a few moments each day.

Silence will nurture your Soul.

Breathe into the Silence and feel your Heart expanding in Love and Joy.

Relax
Sleep
Heal

Be mindful
Be quiet
Be YOU

Connecting with your Angels

Today, take a few minutes -10 or 15- to sit comfortably and quietly.

Breathe in Silence. Breathe in Life. Expand your heart and invite your Guardian Angel to join you.

When you are quiet, you can listen to your Angels! Now... ask your Angel a question and listen... in Silence.

When you finish, thank your Angel and write the message below.

Date:

Chapter 4

Connect - We are One

My beautiful Spark of Divine Light,

We are here to help you in any endeavour your Soul desires to sail. Remember to ask us for help and guidance.

We are surrounding you with Divine Love and Healing Light.

You are safe.

You are Loved.

As you increase your connection with Source and the Divine, this connection will open new paths in your Life.

Live your Life.

Life is beautiful!

Beautiful is the Service you can make your World and Mother Earth by opening your Heart and your mind!

Find new ways of connecting with Gaia. She loves you! Nature is Divine. Nature is God-Creation. Find God/Goddess/Source, in Nature. Find yourself in Nature!

Look after your Natural world. You are made of a deep Loving Nature. You belong to the Divine and to Gaia, Mother Earth.

Connect…

When you finally feel as ONE, you will realise that there is NO separation. You are ONE. Feel the Divine, Gaia and yourself as ONE.

Then, the illumination will come. That's all about it. You simple KNOW that you are ONE.

You are the river, the sea, the trees, the flowers, the mountains, the wind, the clouds, the fire, the Love, the Divine!

This is the truth we are telling you.

Open your wings, let yourself fly, feel the wind in your face, feel your Soul filled with Joy!

Feel

Fly

Joy

You are here to be happy. Nothing is a struggle except in your mind. Move into your Heart and you will feel Peace and you will be Happy.

Let your worries out of your Life. Give them to us, your Celestial friends and carers. We love you so much… Call upon us, your Angels, and you will feel how we take out your worries and burdens away. You will immediately feel the shift of energy in you! Try it!

Connecting with your Angels

Today, I invite you to draw yourself, and around you, draw Mother Nature. It could be a river, some trees, flowers, clouds, animals, anything that you relate to!

Above you, draw the Divine. There is no right or wrong way of seeing It. It could be Angels, Sparks of Light, a Bird… allow yourself to connect and open to your personal creativity! Ask your angels to be by your side!

Colour in this page and draw a Love Heart around your picture. YOU ARE ALL ONE!

Date:

Chapter 5

A message from Blue Angel

Since the storm is gone, now is the time to relax and to open your chakras to receive Divine Guidance.

You are surrounded by incredibly wise Beings of Light who will guide you in writing your book… or in doing whatever your heart dreams of…

These Beings of Light have been with you since a long time ago and now you are ready to start this task:

Write Divine Messages channelled by you with our Divine Help, to help yourself and to help others who may need wise words to walk on this Earth.

Keep opening your Crown Chakra so We can download messages through you to share with others.

For this you must be very balanced and calm. Focus your attention on your heart and let Us guide you with our messages.

We are working together in this book and by the end of it, you will be ready, your dream will be ready, you will take your book out to the World to be shared with so many people who need to listen to our Celestial messages!

We love you so much… and we care for your dreams.

We are here to help you achieve your dreams.

You only need to Ask and Trust.

Today, **BLUE ANGEL** is giving you this message:

YOU ARE NOT ALONE. MILLIONS OF LIGHTS ARE HERE TO PROTECT YOU. THIS IS NOT A

DREAM, MY DEAR. YOU ARE AS AWAKE AS ANYONE ELSE WHO CAN CONTACT ANGELS. YOU JUST NEED TO TRUST.

T o
R ecognise
U niqueness
S ense
T oday
Is the big challenge for you

"Uniqueness sense today" means you live only in TODAY

TODAY only makes sense
TODAY only is unique
LIVE TODAY
That makes sense!

Do not worry for tomorrow or next week, or next year.

Breathe deeply and focus your attention on TODAY, on the NOW. That's all you need to do.

TOMORROW will unfold as it has to.

TOMORROW is not here.

TOMORROW is always tomorrow.

That is why TOMORROW never exists. It is always a possibility in the future.

What future?

The Future you are creating in your mind.

Bring your mind, your consciousness, your attention, your body and your feelings to TODAY.

Breathe deeply.

Breathe TODAY.

Now you can relax and feel your Divine Presence connecting with you.

You are not alone.

Let your Divine Presence, your I AM, guide you.

Feel your Divine Presence in each TODAY of your Life.

Open your heart, and your mind will follow.

Love. Love. Love.

Trust. Trust. Trust.

Clear your throat so you can clear your mind.

Let the burdens go away.

Do not hold onto past hurts.

Forgive. Love. Forget.

It is essential that you clarify your feelings to live in Peace.

When you know exactly how you feel, your mind relaxes and your heart opens to new possibilities.

CHANGE is the magick word. Do not hold into routines that make you feel safe. Feel safe?

No! Go and Change!

Change your plans

Change your hair

Change your moods

Change your expectations

CHANGE is the key to develop yourself into what you feel is right FOR YOU.

BLUE is strength and courage.

Dress in Blue.

Think in Blue.

Live in Blue.

And your Life will turn into your real dream… or your dream will turn, show up into your Life!

A dream where you achieve all you wish for.

A dream you can share with others.

A dream to help our Earth, Gaia, feel better.

A dream where you can help others heal.

A dream…

Your Dream.

Dare to Dream.

Dream your Life… in Blue!

You can do it! I know!

Blue Angel

Connecting with your Angels

The invitation today is for you to dress in Blue! Invite Blue Angel to be with you.

CHANGE is the magick word. Embrace Change. It is ok to Change! Even if it is a small change. Nothing stays the same, everything in this Universe changes.

What can *you* change in your Life to make it better, to feel happier?

Ask your Angel and write the answers here.

Date:

Chapter 6

Live your Life with Red Passion

Today you will work with **Red** Angel. This Angel brings passion, love, interest, enthusiasm and happiness to your Life.

Light a red candle and invoke Red Angel to fill your projects with passion and enthusiasm.

Let Red Angel inject a loving strong energy that will uplift your energy levels, so you can commit to your plans and take guided action to achieve your goals.

Call Red Angel

Think in Red

Red is Passion

Let Passion into your Life

Live a Red Life!

You do not need to worry how you will achieve your goals. Be clear when you set them, then ask Red Angel to come and fill your goals with its powerful energy!

You will see that you achieve your goals, your dreams, much faster if you invoke Red Angel, a passionate 'hard working' Angel.

Breathe deeply and listen. There are times when extra help will be needed. Ask Archangel Michael to come and assist you!

Do not be anxious. You are on the right path, so you can't go wrong!

Always look for the Higher Purpose in your plans.

Set your Heart and your mind on this Higher Purpose. In this way, you will easily fulfil your dreams, projects, plans…

Paint your dreams in Red.

Dream in Red and with passion.

Act in a passionate way.

Find the way to your Purpose with Passion.

Live your Purpose in Red.

Surround your plans with Red Wings.

Imagine you have Red Wings… and FLY!

Red Angel tells you:

"Call upon me when you need that bit of extra help to add passion to your dreams. Sit quietly and breathe deeply. Visualise or see yourself surrounded by my red wings, encouraging you to take that

step, to follow your dream with… passion. See yourself taking that step! Feel it!".

Connecting with your Angels

Today, write a list of those dreams, projects, or desires that you feel need some Passion to become real and manifested.

Get a red colour pencil, pen or crayon and draw Red Angel Wings around your list.

Ask Red Angel to help you trust that your dreams will manifest, if they are for your Highest Good. Smile 😊

Date:

Chapter 7

Trust and Change

Your Life has been blessed with many wonderful moments, people, places and learning experiences. Even if you do not see it sometimes!

It is important that you focus on developing these learnings, and dive deeper and deeper into your Soul. This is the only way you can truly understand why you are here on Earth.

At the same time, the connection with your Higher Self will develop into a close connection with God/Goddess - The Universe and the Divine Intelligence.

You know you are a Healer.

Trust yourself.

We angels need you as an Earth Angel, to assist and help people who need to see to believe.

We will work through you to do miracles in people's lives. But you first need to Trust yourself.

We are speaking about that Trust that is seated deeper into your Heart and your Soul. The Trust that is an Inner Knowing.

You are assisted by the Highest Light Beings in your healing work.

We told you that there were going to be profound changes in your Life.

Now is the Time.

Be ready to immerse yourself in those changes.

Your Life will be brighter and happier. You will bring happiness to yourself and to those who surround and trust you.

In this time of Self-healing, remember you can always ask for Divine Help. Archangel Raphael is here, too! Let us help you. We will answer your prayers happily and readily.

Connect with God, the Archangels and your Angels every time you remember to do so. It will come naturally one day… you will see us and work with us as part of your Team.

Step into your Soul's desires.

Desire only the Highest Good for

you and for others.

Open your Heart, your wings and

your messages to the World.

We are assisting you each time you pray, meditate and breathe deeply. Each time you think of others, or you involve in healing practices, you call upon us for assistance and guidance.

Offer a healing every day. Whatever way you prefer to do it. Listen to someone in need, smile to a stranger who seems sad, use your Reiki hands and your crystals, read a spiritual book to a person who needs company, cook your food with Love. There are so many ways to heal!

Set yourself a time to do so.

You will see that soon this will become a part of the real YOU. And then you will finally Trust us, yourself and the Divine Energy that loves and heals.

It is time for a break.

Give us your worries and let us help you.

Start your practice… Enjoy… Trust…

You are not alone.

You are with God/Great Spirit/Universe.

You are with the Angels!

Connecting with your Angels

Today, I invite you to reflect in which ways you can start healing yourself and others.

Tick from this list the ways you prefer and add some extra ones… from your heart.

Crystal healing

Reiki

Massage

Kinesiology

Active Listening

Mindfulness practice

Meditation

Angel cards reading

Shamanic practices

Walk in Nature

Consciously eating/cooking

Wake up with a smile

Write a Gratitude Journal

Sing happy songs

Sit in Silence

Add more healing practices you may like to try!

_____
_____
_____
_____
_____
_____
_____
_____
_____
_____
_____
_____

Date:

Chapter 8

Draw your Dreams

My dear Earth Angel,

Sit back and relax while I give you a message that will bring Light to your path and will calm your worries.

Close your eyes. Breathe deeply. Can you feel we are here with you? Leave your mind; breathe deeply and focus on your body, on your senses… Can you feel us now?

Listen to the silence. Enjoy the sound of the Universe in your Heart.

There has never been a better time for you to start this project.

Remember to Trust yourself. We are helping you because you have asked for Divine Guidance and Help.

Step by step. Sometimes slowly, sometimes faster.

Enjoy the process. Step by step.

If you start feeling anxious or nervous, stop.

Breathe deeply and stay balanced. This will move the surrounding energies faster for you to achieve your dreams.

You will be surprised by all the changes that you will awaken to… soon. Marvellous changes that will nurture your Heart, your Soul and your Life!

Get clearer and clear your picture, your dreams. Write them down, clearly. We are working for and with you to achieve them… for your Highest Good.

As we said, focus on TODAY…

Focus on your BREATH

Focus on what you WANT

Draw your dreams…

Use Divine Energy…

… Colour them with Love,

Trust,

Peace,

Compassion…

And BELIEVE!!!

They will be real as soon as you Trust yourself.

Enjoy…!

Love…!

Live…

In Joy!

We will never be tired of reminding you….

TRUST YOURSELF

And ASK for DIVINE HELP!

The Universe Loves you and supports your DREAMS.

DREAM... with Love

Connecting with your Angels

Today, I invite you to get all your colours, paints, pencils or crayons ready and to draw your DREAM.

How does your DREAM look like? Be audacious, let yourself dream BIG!

While you do this activity, I suggest you listen to any of these Alexia Chellun songs:

1. The power is Here Now
2. Take your Destiny
3. Allowing
4. Trust
5. Abundance

When you finish, 'show' your dream to your Angels and ask them to bring it forth if it is for your Highest Good. TRUST that they will deliver... this or something better!

Date:

Chapter 9

Intuition - Gratitude - Love

It is in difficult times when you must strengthen your Faith in Us. God/Universe or the Divine, Archangels and Angels are here to protect and guard you. We love you and we will be pleased to help you if you ask.

Close your eyes. Stay still. Breathe deeply. Feel our Presence close to you. You are never alone. Connect with your Spiritual side more often.

Help your Soul grow.

Read books that help you increase your Spiritual Life.

You deserve to live an abundant life.

No one wants to live in misery. Not you. Ask for Abundance in all areas of your Life: health, love, relationships, well-being, finances!

If you *feel* you are abundant you will be more likely to give to others: help, time, Love, guidance, support.

Breathe deeply and open your heart to receiving. As you receive, start giving… from your Heart.

Abundance is Infinite! It is always flowing. That is why you have to give! To keep receiving!

The more Love you give, the more Love you will receive.

The more Time you give, the more time you will have.

The more Help you give, the more help you will receive!

There is always time for MORE in the Abundance frequency.

Ask. Trust. Receive. Give. Love. Breathe.

We are guiding you right now to manifest your deepest, inner desires. Listen to your heart. Follow your dreams and your intuition. What resonates with you is the right thing FOR YOU.

Trust your guts, your feelings and your intuition.

This is another way we are communicating with you and if you listen attentively, you will not only find yourself in your path on Earth, but you will also be connected to Heaven's energy!

Being connected to Heaven, or God, or the Universe or the Divine, will allow you to download the information to need as a Light Worker.

We know how deeply you enjoy learning, connecting with the Celestial Realm and helping others!

Now, clearly ask what your heart desires.

You will definitely be receiving it.

Trust that is already on your way.

Develop your connection with God/Goddess, Archangels, Angels and Guides, more and more every day.

We are enthusiastically awaiting that time of each day when you call upon us for help, messages and healing.

We lovingly welcome your requests, and we answer them promptly. It's our Divine task!

If there are times that you feel your prayers are not being answered, then tune more deeply, calm your mind, connect with your heart, clear your Crown chakra and feel, listen to our answers.

You may not receive the answer you want. But rest assured that you WILL be receiving AN ANSWER! Listen carefully. Listen with your heart, with your Soul, with Love…

There will be other times when we can give you what you ask for 'on the spot'!

Remember there is a Divine Timing that may differ from your Earthly time. Actually, it differs! Which does not mean you won't receive but you may receive in a more appropriate time, or you may receive in a different way than the one you requested. Whatever and whenever you receive it is always for your Highest Good. Keep this in mind.

When you receive, remember to be grateful, as Gratitude nurtures the connection channel between you and Us.

When you are grateful, your Heart chakra vibrates in a loving pattern that we LOVE!

Be grateful and feel it in your Heart. Notice how deeply you breathe, how your heart expands, and how your own energy increases!

We Love you and we wish you well. All the changes you are living today are leading you to your Lightworker's path.

Always choose Love. Tune into "Love I found", as Doreen taught you!

Love is such a High-Level Energy frequency that gives you –and whoever feels it in its pure essence- the ability to heal.

Make TO LOVE your main purpose in LIFE and your LIFE will unfold as you want.

Love Heals Life.

Connecting with your Angels

This practice is about clarifying YOUR giving and receiving creation and manifestation.

1. What does your intuition tell you about *Giving*?
2. What can you GIVE freely and unconditionally? Write 3 things inside the stars:

1. What does your intuition tell you about *Receiving*?
2. What would you like to RECEIVE? Write 3 things and remember to receive with Grace and Gratitude!

Date:

Chapter 10

Regain your power! Angel wings box

Finally, you are here!

When turbulent times surround you, please remember there is a place within you that only you have access to: your HEART.

Ignore all your thoughts from your mind.

Bring your focus to your heart.

Move your energy and attention from your mind down to your Heart chakra, in the middle of your chest.

This will calm your mind and will help you take distance from the 'turbulence'.

Ask us Angels and Guides to surround you with our loving wings and to protect you. Feel our warm energy around you. Stay focused on your heart.

We are here to help you stay balanced and pass through any storm in your life with no harm.

Breathe deeply

Exhale slowly

Again – Again – Again

If there is any other worry or concern that you didn't write and burnt earlier in the Ceremony, and it's now in your mind, please give it to us.

Imagine you are putting all your worries and concerns in a treasure box. A box with wings. Angel wings!

Ask us, your Angels, to take the box out to the Universe. There, your worries and concerns will be transmuted into loving, clear, healthy, balanced energy.

The Universe is Perfect

You are Perfect

Connect with Perfection and feel it in your body, in your heart, in your aura, inside you, around you. Feel yourself Perfect!

Breathe in deeply. Feel and be grateful for your perfection. Exhale slowly. Relax.

Do not give anyone or anything the power that it is inside you.

Stay centered

Stay focused

Stay balanced

Regain your power

Now imagine White Light coming down from the Universe. Surround yourself with this bright, clear, loving White Light.

Imagine this light as a pillar around you. You are there, in the middle of this pillar. Feel the Light becoming stronger and stronger, brighter and brighter, all around you.

Nothing can trespass your Pillar.

You are protected!

You are safe!

Ask your Guardian Angels for help if you feel to do so. They are here with their loving, caring energy…

Breathe in deeply

Smile

Relax

You are protected

We now ask Archangel Michael to surround you with his royal blue energy. Imagine Archangel Michael in front of you, behind you and on your sides. He can be with many people simultaneously.

Feel the power and strength of this powerful Archangel protecting you. Nothing but LOVE can trespass this energy. Rest assured that He is always protecting you.

Connecting with your Angels

Today we invite you to do a special activity. You are going to create your own Angel box!

Get a cardboard box, or any other kind of box, small to medium size, and cover it with wrapping paper, or paint it the colours you prefer.

Once it is ready, you will add some angel wings. Go out and find feathers! The feathers that are sold in craft shops are also useful and colourful! Add a few feathers to the top of your box or draw an angel if you prefer!

Play some calming music and find a place where you can be by yourself for a few minutes.

Celebrate your creation, ask your angels to bless your angel box and TRUST that they will help you!

As worries come to your mind, or appear in your life, write them down and place them in your Angel Box, saying:

"Dear Angels, take this worry away, clear it from my mind, dissolve its energy and take it to the Light for transformation and transmutation."

Then breathe in deeply and feel your Perfection. You are perfect as you are now! Smile!

This is my Angelbox.

When it is full, I offer the worries to the spirit of Fire for complete release.

Chapter 11

Rainbow Angel wants to join you today

This is Rainbow Angel message for you:

There are some days when your energy level may drop, you feel down, slow or sad. You see your world in black.

There are other days when you feel shining, happy for no reason, euphoric, boosting energy, you want to run or to fly!

And there are some other days when you feel like a Rainbow! All the colours, emotions and wonderful feelings fill you, your Life, your activities and your dreams!

These are the best and most balanced days, when you can do anything to turn your dreams, your purpose, your Project into action and reality.

Red action… ready, full or energy to act!

Orange… dare to dream!

Yellow… shine! Take control!

Green… heart, Love, Love yourself

Love others
Love what you do
Love what you have
Love what you are
Love Gaia
Love Angels!
Love the Divine Essence
In you

Blue… start to communicate clearly

Indigo… take a step further and let your intuition guide you

Violet… connect with your intuition, with the Universe, Love your Life, feel safe. You are supported and guided.

The Rainbow Angel loves to surround you with its colours, energy and Love.

Let It Be
Let Yourself Be
Let Love Be

Listen to the music in your heart.

Breathe in the smell of roses and jasmines.

Feel the Rainbow Energy all around you.

Touch the colours. Imagine their texture.

Ground yourself in a pillar of White Light and let Rainbow Angel shine its colours upon you!

Yes. You know it: YOU ARE THE TREASURE! (THE RAINBOW!)

I Love you
Rainbow Angel

Connecting with your Angels

Today, we invite you to draw or paint a rainbow! Over each colour of your rainbow, write a dream or a project that you want to manifest and live. Or you can write and give thanks for your Blessings!

Under the rainbow, write your name in rainbow colours, or glue a photo of yourself. Let the energy of the Rainbow surround and bless you. Be playful! Have fun!

Date:

Chapter 12

Angel Colours

We are delighted that you are taking this time to channel our messages. We have been waiting for this moment for so long…!

We love you, _____ (write your name on the line)

We respect you for WHO you ARE

We know you are a wonderfully gifted Child of God/Universe/Divine.

We trust you will deliver our messages purely, with a soulful intention, to help others on this Earthly journey and beyond!

Let us introduce ourselves: We are the

ANGEL COLOURS

We are Infinite. There are so many of us as there are colours, shapes and grades…

When we get together, all our colours and energies become White.

White Angel, along with Silver and Golden Angels, are the Highest and more powerful Angels.

Their Divine Energy sums up all the other Divine Energies and colours!

You can play with us, invoke us and make plans with us! We are here to help YOU.

As you know, you (and all humans) have free will and we respect this.

Please, ask us for help and we will be with you, helping, guiding, protecting and bathing you with the colour energy you need.

White Angel is here to Love you Unconditionally

Whenever you need help with:

- ❖ Health
- ❖ Solving problems
- ❖ Calming you (or others)
- ❖ Finding Peace
- ❖ Love and Relationships

invoke White Angel

and imagine I am surrounding you with my wings, in a Celestial hug and bathing you in Divine White Light and Energy.

Close your eyes now. Feel the energy all around you. Breathe this energy in. Relax. Trust that I am here with you to protect and help you.

Golden Angel…

Will assist you when you call upon it.

Its mission is to bring Peace to any situation, person, and to help Mother Earth in these times when She is struggling to support you and overcome all the damage and pain being caused to Her.

Invoke Golden Angel and ask to surround, wrap Gaia, Earth, in Golden Light. Imagine Mother Earth in a Golden caring energy cloud. Send this Light into her core, into her Heart. Feed Gaia with Golden Angel's Energy. She will be so grateful…

When you feel the need of Peace, ask Golden Angel to come and help you. It will be delighted to assist!

Artist: Silvana Tempestini

Other situations may need you to invoke… **Silver Angel**

This is an Angel with bubbly energy that will attend immediately to your request for help. It specialises in lifting moods, relaxing a tense situation during grieving times, if you are sad or melancholic, stressed, worried or unhappy.

Call upon Silver Angel and receive its Silver Energy that will shift your energy and transmute into a Higher Vibrational frequency that will make you feel happy from inside out.

Silver Angel loves dancing! Do you like dancing?

Connecting with your Angels

There will be Light today! Get your candles ready! Gold, Silver and White candles, each representing one Angel.

Once you have your candles, make it a ritual to start or end your day connecting with these angels. Find a quiet and comfortable space, light the 3 candles, and invoke Gold, Silver and White angels to your side. Then, ask Them for the assistance you need!

Write here any messages or guidance you receive from Them.

When you finish, as you blow the candles, see the smoke taking your worries away to the Universe for transformation and transmutation.

Always remember to give Thanks! to your angels.

Date:

Chapter 13

Green Angel, Healing Angel

Feel a healing vibration through your body. It is like a wave of energy coming from your Crown Chakra on top of your head, down through your neck, your torso, your body, your legs… and grounding you on Earth.

It's me… Green Angel! Every time you take a deep breath in and focus on green colour, you will be calling me.

When I reach your vibrational state is when you feel the wave of healing energy. A wave of Green Light, a wave of Love, of Health, of Warmth…

Green Angels are assisting Archangel Raphael on his Healing mission. When someone calls upon Archangel Raphael, we also hear the call and we come along!

If you see sparks of Green Light, it is us that are assisting you as well.

Whenever you feel:
Tired
Sick
Sad
Exhausted
Overwhelmed
Depressed
Burnt out
In pain
Lonely

Remember to call us, the Green Angels and give us your pain, your health concern, your emotional hurt… we reassure you will start feeling better straight away.

We will take care of your physical, emotional, spiritual and mental pain if you ask for our assistance!

Close your eyes. Imagine yourself walking into a warm, clear ocean. You are surrounded by pristine waters. Jump into the wave! Take a deep breath in, feel our green shining presence clearing and washing your pain and unwanted thoughts and emotions, which are the cause of your situation.

You are perfect, whole and healthy…

We are here to help you recover this feeling of being healthy and happy.

Each time you swim into a wave, a wave of water that purifies, a wave of energy that heals, a green wave through which Green Angels bath you in health, calm and peaceful energies, you ARE feeling better and better and your body, mind and Soul start shining with White and Green Light.

This will raise your vibration, taking you into a higher vibrational estate that aligns you with your Divine Presence and the Universe …

Float in a Green Wave of Energy…

Green Angels are surrounding you!

Connecting with your Angels

Today, we invite you to play "Mozart by the Sea" Piano Concerto Piano Concerto No. 20 and Romance No. 21 - II Andante.

The links below will take you to this healing, calming, expanding music.

https://www.youtube.com/watch?v=Mwzz2NLYztA

https://www.youtube.com/watch?v=lYD7XtqUgeo

Allow yourself time to breath, float in green healing energy and relax.

Date:

Chapter 14

You know this one... Purple Angel!

Hola, my beloved Earth Angel! It's so good to contact you today!

Purple is the colour of the Sacred, the Priests and Priestesses of Light, the Colour of Transmutation, the Violet Flame.

Surround yourself in purple wings when you feel you need to change your energies, or you want to transmute a situation, a feeling, a thought or a behaviour.

Purple Angels work closely with the Violet Flame of Transmutation and we can help you re-generate and turn your worries into positive outcomes!

Call upon us when you decide that you no longer wish to be immersed in fear, worries, anger, resentment, self-doubt, harsh self-talk or actions that you are not happy with.

We will come with our wings wide opened and embrace you with Purple Light.

Feel the warmth of our Purple energy in your heart and around your body.

Imagine yourself sending your cares through our wings to Heavens, and in return, hundreds of Purple Angels will bring peace, compassion and forgiveness into your heart and Life.

Breathe in these loving feelings.

Breathe them deeply.

Feel them in your heart.

Let them become part of you.

You are loving, caring and beautiful. This is how we see you! This is YOU!

Imagine many of us, Purple Angels, around you, sending you Purple Light, Love and an Infinite sense of Peace, Inner Peace.

We are here with you.

You only need to ASK for our presence and help.

We reassure you there is no situation that cannot be transmuted into Love if you have our Celestial help!

Purple hugs for you, my dear…

And Thanks for calling us!

Connecting with your Angels

Today, Purple Angel invites you to write here a list of your worries, concerns and situations, thoughts and emotions that you wish to heal, balance and transform.

Then, draw purple wings around your list. Be creative! Have fun!

Take a deep breath in. Invoke Purple Angel to help you in the transformation of what is in your list. Ask this powerful angel to bring forth Purple Light of Love, Inner Peace and Positive Changes.

Breathe deeply. Allow yourself to be helped! Trust!

Date:

Chapter 15

I am here... don't be afraid

I am here, dear one. Some people fear me because of my colour. But there is no reason for this.

I am Black Angel. Yes, I am Black. But my energies are not to be feared. I am here to absorb any energy that no longer serves your Highest Good, and to take it to the Light.

I am the Angel of Transitions: from a stage in your Life, to the other; when you go through big changes (and there were, are and will be changes in your Life!); when you close one door and look and wait for another to open...

I am with you in all these moments in your Life.

Do not fear me, my beloved one. I am from the Light. And like all the other Angels, I have a mission! Mine is to support you when you are travelling through Changes, to take your old energies to the Light, so you can have space, energetic space, for the upcoming steps in your Life.

And I LOVE YOU.

Close your eyes. Take a deep breath in and imagine I am surrounding you with my wings. I have special wings that can receive your negative or unwanted energies without harm, and at the same time, I release new, transformed, Love-filled energies into your aura, your body and your emotions.

These new energies are powerful, strong and loving. Feel yourself regenerated energetically. Step into your Power now!

You are renewed. With these new energies you are now ready to move on confidently, knowing that new doors are ready to be opened by YOU, ready to be able to SEE those new doors, with the courage to open them!

Take a deep breath in again and step forward. You are strong and capable. Go for it! You are not alone!

All my Love,

Black Angel

Connecting with your Angels

For this connection practice, draw two doors on a piece of paper, one next to the other, leaving a gap in between them.

On the left door, write the situations, people, emotions that you are ready to let go, that no longer serve your Highest Good. Everything that you want to let go, place it to the door. Then, use black colour to cover over your words. The door is closed.

Next, on the right door, write the experiences, projects, people, that you are willing to connect with and bring into your Life. Use bright colours and fancy writing! The door is now open for you!

Now, draw yourself in between the doors. Close one door and then open the other one. Behind you, during this exercise, is Black Angel, holding space for the Change! All is well. All will be well. Trust.

Date:

Chapter 16

An Angel from the Sea

Greetings to you, Sweet Soul…

Let me introduce myself, I am Turquoise Angel.

Yes, I am a strange colour. But I really enjoy being different! My energy is light, it flows freely like a river, it is smooth as a caress, kind as a breeze…

Your energy can be like mine! Yes! Light, soft, delicate. Tune into Turquoise colour! Can you see it? Can you imagine it? It's the colour of the sky, of the sea, of the eyes of a person; it is the colour of pristine waters, forming clouds and distinguished flower Jade Vine. This is ME. Turquoise Angel.

I will surround you with my energy if you ask me. Take a deep breath in and imagine yourself floating in a clean, transparent, pure turquoise sea. Feel yourself, your body, your heart and your emotions becoming lighter and lighter while you float, maybe swim, in my sea.

Inhale this calming and gentle energy very deeply. Let it be part of your heart and your Soul. Let it surround your thoughts, your emotions and your body, too.

Let me hold you as the water holds and wraps you when you float. Let yourself go. You are safe. You are transparent. You are calm.

You are now changing your energy field. You are now light, kind, smooth…

I touched your Heart with Love. Accept my gift of Love and Sweetness. Open your Heart to receive them and to connect with my Turquoise energy. It is all yours now.

Float, swim or fly! You are lighter, clean, lively, liberated! You are also safe and protected.

I wrap my wings around your Heart, and I assure you that being lighter and happier is OK for you! You are safe.

Turquoise breeze to your heart from

Turquoise Angel

Connecting with your Angels

I invite you today to go to a place where there is water. It could be a river, the ocean, a lake, a stream of water, or a swimming pool! If you can't find such a place, don't worry! You can get into the shower!

Once you are close -or in- the water, close your eyes and ask Turquoise Angel to surround you. Feel the water flowing all over you as the angel's wings embrace. Let Turquoise Angel surround you and give all your worries to it. Enjoy this time in the water… with this calming Angel! Remember to take deep breaths… slowly… relaxing… Enjoy!

Then write here how you felt before and after this practice.

Date:

Chapter 17

Your essence: Freedom, Joy & Love

In the air… in the slightly felt air around you is where you can find us. Air is our place of connection. Sit still and you will feel us. A soft caress, a gentle vibration, a spark of Light, a calm melody, a singing bird, a profound feeling of being Home. Here we are. Notice Us. We only want you to be free, happy and joyful. This is your true purpose in Life… Everything else is only a meaning to achieve your Purpose.

You came here to Earth to experience Freedom, Joy, Growth and Love.

Remember you are already all these. Freedom, Joy, Growth and Love.

You came here to *re-member*. To gather experiences together, to design a bigger and deeper picture, a closer connection with your Soul.

All these words that we have offered you intend to help you re-connect with your Essence. They are only a guide for you. You can re-create these ideas, change them and even create new ones! New ideas and new messages!

Coming back Home is a Journey. A deliciously challenging Journey. Learn as much as you can. Love as much as you can. Feed and nurture your Soul. Make a difference in your own Life. You know you came here to start –or continue- a path of intensive spiritual learning and We would love to help you and be by your side if you allow and invite us to this Journey.

The most important thing We want you to know, feel and live is to TRUST.

TRUST in yourself

TRUST in your Angels

TRUST in your Spirit Guides and Animal Guides

TRUST your feelings

TRUST your intuition

TRUST your Heart

It is a day-to-day experience.

It is a moment – now awareness

It is a "Here I am, Life!"

It is a wonderful, magickal Life…

when you TRUST!

And you ask: "How do I trust?"

We smile at that question for it is a Universal human question.

If you are here now it is because you have trusted before.

We can help you re-member.

TRUST is that inner knowing…

Calming feeling

Deep breath that you take

That inner smile

TRUST is to let go of expectations, for when you TRUST, amazing things happen, greater things than what you expect will manifest in your Life.

TRUST in your dreams. Your sleeping dreams. We give you messages that if you listen and pay attention to, will guide you to achieve your desires and your desires for Happiness, Love, Peace and Contentment.

Breathe deeply and expand your heart.

Relax

Stay still

Breathe deeply again

Fill your heart with Love

Smile

Be aware of your thoughts

Create a new thought now. A thought of TRUST.

"I Trust"

"I Trust the Universe"

"I am Open and I Trust"

Connect often to your Angels and Guides.

Speak to Us like you speak to your most trusted friend. Feel our presence. Listen to what We tell you… with your heart.

There is nothing to be afraid of. All is well.

It is all organised in a way that Life will take you to the next level if you allow it!

TRUST – We say

How do I Trust? – You ask

Say "I TRUST"

Repeat "I TRUST"

Say "I TRUST" and breathe deeply. Exhale slowly and smile!

Feel the TRUST coming into your heart.

Stop your thinking now!!!

Feel your heart. Feel the Love and Peace and Calm you experience when you say, "I TRUST" and you open your heart.

Say "I TRUST" and let go of expectations and thoughts. Sit in the feeling of "I TRUST" and let your Guides and Angelic Team help you.

If you say "Thank you" we will know that you are allowing Us to help you and that you are open to receiving what you asked for... or something better!!

Connecting with your Angels

Do you like crystals? The invitation today is to connect with a blue crystal. Blue crystals -in all its shades- are the crystals of Trust.

Lapis Lazuli, Blue Kyanite, Celestite, Sapphire... wear them as a pouch or bracelet, in a pendant, place one in your pocket, or under your pillow.

Let the energy of the Crystals and angels embrace you!

Remember Archangel Michael's energy is Blue!

Date:

Chapter 18

Allow the messages in

Use colour, sound, light, vibration and fragrances. Mix any colour with a sound… bells, drums, music, your own voice, Nature's sounds.

Bring Light from the Universe to surround you. You are now in a Pillar of Light, White Light, healing and protecting Light.

What's your favourite smell? Bring it to your experience now… essential oils, Nature, flames… or maybe food!

Clear your heart, your inner space. Make it Sacred.

Ask Archangel Michael for protection.

Now, combine your chosen colour with the sound and the fragrance.

Fill your heart with them.

Bath your sacred inner space with them.

Breathe deeply, slowly… Ask. Allow. TRUST. Feel how your heart expands.

We know you are listening.

Tune in!

Put the volume up (you do this by slowing down)

What do you hear? Can you listen?

You can ask for clear action steps to be shown to you.

One step at a time.

Take that step.

Start walking.

TRUST.

You are now moving forward.

Feel Gratitude in your heart.

Ask Us angels for your next step.

Allow the message in.

Follow it.

TRUST.

Can you see how TRUST works?

Be mindful, or write, your TRUST experiences, as in the acknowledging of these experiences, you teach your heart (and mind) to TRUST more and more, and there will then be more magickal experiences delivered into your Life. YOU will CREATE those experiences!

TRUST.

We love you and we are here with you

Your Guardian Angel

and some more Angels

Connecting with your Angels

This is your TRUST list!

As more and more synchronicities show up in your Life, write here your magickal experiences.

Chapter 19

Expand your heart

Make it fun.

Don't take Life so seriously

Relax

All is well

Smile

Do you know that Life is meant to be LIVED?

Live your Life

Enjoy your Life

Love your Life

Being Grateful opens doors...

Be grateful

Say "Thank you" often

Give thanks from your heart

Appreciate what you have, what you do

and what you ARE.

Be grateful for all that you have, all that you do, and all that you ARE!

You are Lovable

You are Beautiful

You are Magickal

You are Powerful

You are Unique

Tap into your Inner Wisdom.

Realise that you are not alone.

Call your Celestial Helpers to come along and help you enjoy your Life.

Challenges help you grow. Stay with Joy and the challenges will become a marvellous growing Journey for your Soul.

Remember that your Soul needs these challenges to grow, to expand, to re-member, to heal, to awaken…

Live your challenges as if you are helping a dearest friend through a challenging situation…

Be patient
Be loving
Be calm
Be nurturing

With yourself!
With your Soul!
With your Journey!
With your Heart!

There is nothing that us, Angels, can say to convince you if your heart is not open to the Celestial possibilities.

Embrace your Heart. Put your hands on your chest, over your heart. Take a deep breath in. Slowly… exhale and relax. Imagine your heart opening like a lotus flower or like a beautiful red rose…

Opening. Opening. Opening.

Take another deep breath in and on the exhale –slowly- expand your Heart, your loving energies.

Expanding. Expanding. Expanding.

FEEL the new feeling!

Stay with it!

Feel. Open. Expand. Love. Enjoy. Relax.

Do this process every time you feel tense, doubtful, stressed... The more often you do this process, the more your heart will expand, trust and relax. It will become natural for you to have an open, expanded heart and loving emotions... at any moment!

Bring this process into your awareness and practice it for a few days, notice how your heart and your emotional body relax, and you will feel more balanced and harmonious within yourself, with others and with your environment.

It is possible!

Make it fun!

Enjoy your Life!

Bring your attention down into your heart. Breathe them. Connect with the FEELING rather than with your thoughts. Again... and again and again. How are you FEELING now?

Feel your heart expanding. Feel the joy. Feel the Love.

Connecting with your Angels

Today, I offer you a challenging invitation!

Sit, meditate and reflect. Ask your Angels for help and guidance. Post them these questions:

How can I open my heart?

What can I do to enjoy my Life?

How can I love my Life?

What do I need to feel now?

Write the answers you received here:

Date:

Chapter 20

Walking with you... always

Dear Soul Seeker and Angel Lover,

In closing, we invite you to place this book in a special place where you can come to us often. On your altar, your bedside table, your reading desk…

Once you have read all our words, come back, hold this book in your hands, place it on your heart, close your eyes and connect again with the Angels. Then ask them mentally (or out loud!) to give you a message —or an Angel- that you need for this moment in life and open this book randomly.

The message will be here for you!

TRUST (again) that you will be shown the perfect message that you need to read,

the right actions to follow,

the colours to work with.

Read. Do. Act. Feel! Live! Love!

You can, at other times, and if you wish, refer to the 'Messages' (Content page) and scroll down with your finger or your eyes until a message comes to your attention. TRUST (once again!) that these will be the right words that you need to 'hear' and read at that moment.

Hold this book close to your heart.

Take a deep breath in. Delve deep into your own heart.

Imagine Us, Angels, are pouring these messages into your heart.

Do not worry about nor intend to remember the words.

Inhale the ENERGY of the messages that you have already read.

We Angels bathe your Heart and Soul with loving energies and vibrations.

TRUST.

We are deeply grateful that you connected with us and shared and read our messages.

We wish that you could hear our words being whispered in your ears, your heart and your Life.

Know that we Love you as you are a Divine Spark of Light and that is how We see you.

Call upon Us, your Celestial Helpers, and we will be with you. No waiting!

Vibrate with sound.

Surround yourself with Angels.

Bathe your Life in colours.

Let us hold your hand and, step by step, walk this Journey with you.

For Peace is coming to Earth. One person at a time. Starting with YOU. YOU are important.

Find Peace within your heart first. The rest will follow…

Live your Life with Love and Peace. Peace in your mind and Love in your heart.

You are Safe. You are Loved.

TRUST

SHINE

LOVE

LIVE

You ARE Love.

LOVE always love you! Feel it!

Final words

To YOU, with whom I am connected as you read this book…Thank you!

My hope is that you find in these Angel Messages and Connecting with the Angels practices, the comfort, strength, trust, support, ideas, encouragement and Unconditional Love to connect with the amazing Celestial energy of the Angels! Thank you for being here!

Along with the Angelic Team, there were many people involved in the journey of creating this book.

I would like to thank and acknowledge the first 'push' to learn more profound lessons from the Angels, given by my dearest husband. After reading one of D. Virtue's books, he encouraged -or shall I say 'directed'? - me to join the Angel Intuitive course in Queensland in 2011. I couldn't say 'no', of course! I was so excited! That weekend I discovered a wide window into the Angelic Realm! My husband, my Earth Angel, thank you! Your love, understanding, patience, enthusiasm, support and trust in me got me here!

I want to thank my own Guardian Angels and Spirit Guides for taking me on this challenging, but rewarding and insightful journey of channelling messages and writing them to create this book to share with others. I know you are proud of me. I love you very much and I love sharing my Earthly and Heavenly journey with you, my Celestial Team! You are amazing!

There were many friends whose words of encouragement and support instilled the enthusiasm of moving forward and publishing this book and to whom I am very grateful: Nancy Mattos, Mirjana Bosnovska, Leisa Rodios (my beloved friend from the Other Side) and Silvana Tempestini (my soul-sister and creator of the Golden Angel artwork). Thank you to Christian

Ravello, a creative friend and author, for your patient guidance.

To my dog Cimi, my Celestial Gift sent to me by the Angels many moons ago, who sat quietly next to me for many hours while I was typing, editing and creating this book. You are my Super Girl!

To close this circle of Gratitude, I would like to thank my sweet friend Amy Hillenbrand, who gave the last 'push' and encouragement to publish this book.

I am honoured and grateful to have you all in my life, as you are also part of my amazing Earth Angels Team!

In Gratitude and Love,

Claudia

About the author

Claudia Boymouchakian is a natural Angel Channeller, Reiki Master Teacher, Sound Therapist, Shamanic Practitioner and Healer/Curandera, Metaphysical Teacher, Motivational Speaker, Meditation and Mindfulness teacher, creator of Angelic Connection©, Spiritual Growth Journey©, Shamanic Practitioner Certificate and Shamanic Reiki Programs, among other courses.

As part of her Service to the Light, she channels messages of guidance and inspiration from the Angels and Spirit Guides on her Angelic Sessions.

She has taught classes and offered energy healing and shamanic sessions in Argentina, Brazil, Europe and

Australia and her passion for connecting with Angels and Archangels, Guides and Animal and Spirit Guides, took her to connect with the Celestial Realm and channel this book: "No name. Just Angels!"

Although Claudia loves face to face teaching, she has also designed many online courses, guided by the angels: 14 días de transformación espiritual (in Spanish), Spiritual Growth Journey, Reiki for Animals, Shamanic Practices and Healing Certificate. And there are more courses in the creation cloud… guided by her Team of Angels.

With many decades' experience as a primary and high school teacher and Educational Psychologist, Claudia is now sharing transformational Metaphysical, Angelic, Crystal Power, Shamanic Practices and Reiki, Sound and Energy Healing classes and seminars with people who are learning to 'see beyond the Veil' and who love Angels, Pachamama and a bit of mystery, metaphysics and magick…

Claudia's dream is to empower people worldwide to connect with Angels and Archangels, to trust their own intuition and to take their spiritual practices to new heights and shifts, creating a Peaceful, Loving and

Healthy life. She is doing it for herself and she knows you can create a wonderful Life with the help of the Angelic Realm, too!

Visit Claudia's website and claim your FREE BONUS here:

www.purpleangelhealing.com.au

Stay connected!

FB: Purple Angel Healing Centre | Facebook

Instagram: Claudia B. (@purpleangelhc) • Instagram photos and videos

www.ingramcontent.com/pod-product-compliance
Lightning Source LLC
Chambersburg PA
CBHW062038290426
44109CB00026B/2664